In the Absence of Birds

Ruth C. Chad

Červená Barva Press
Somerville, Massachusetts

Červená Barva Press
P.O. Box 440357
W. Somerville, MA 02144

editor@cervenabarvapress.com
http://www.cervenabarvapress.com

Visit the bookstore at:
http://www.thelostbookshelf.com

Production: Allison O'Keefe
Cover Image: Ruth Chad

ISBN: 978-1-950063-98-7
LCCN: 2024943601

CONTENTS

I: Days of My Mother

II: To Plant a Lupine at Twilight in the
Company of the Earthworm

III: Another Haiku in Summer

For my family:
Mark, Emma, Avi and Simone, whose love and support
have sustained me, and for my parents and brother.

I entered the universal, dazzled and desiring.
-Czeslaw Milosz

In the Absence of Birds

I:

DAYS OF MY MOTHER

Perpetual Twilight

I plunge into the hot space
a monochrome canvas
dumb furniture holds you

In here   time is spent
and spent again
a dull ache   grief throbs

Through the gritty window
an arc of last light
on silver hair

Time presses against your skin
leaving lines
on the papery surface

your hands hang
limp   disfigured
by arthritic nodes

I smooth your sheets   secure
your hearing aid   the last one
lost in a crevice

knit together particles of dust
to make a coat
for your shivering shoulders

January dusk   purple light
the flush of your cheeks fading
into oncoming night

-for my mother

Wind chimes

we bought in Maine
near the sea
where we went to escape

a compass on a chain
a gold disk to catch

the wind and rain
a painted indigo bell

I do not understand this music
amorphous and celestial

If I Had Wings

I

I walk low on a black road
close to wet   yellow leaves
to the scent of regret

I slip on hard memories
curse their fame
avoid a thousand eyes

my feet going
anywhere
that isn't hell

II

Above me wild birds
high   on warm wind
angels on the horizon

if I had wings
I would have risen
early with the birds

easy lift off the lake
I would have taken you with me
into blue light

Light Comes Slowly

-i.m. Morris Chad (1920-2013)

Light comes slowly
in the morning now

the closed   hard sheath
of ashen sky

It was a frigid dawn like this
the day you died

your small   cold body
stiff   wrapped in white sheets

I shivered before you
like a sparrow in snow

As the Light Diminishes

If I could be those brazen birches
lost in tree loud chatter

in the tapping of leaf and branch
roam the forest

where the dirt path
is all a fall

of pine needles
swept by the wind

into soft drifts
I could forget

the harsh grind
of your walker on wood

and the morning call
the wall of disappointment

behind the apartment door
the sad curve

of your mouth
and the sun

sliding under the horizon
as the light diminishes

Haiku in Winter

Resting skin on skin
oranges in the glass bowl

how lonely this day

The Crabapple Tree

From unspoiled soil
still short in the stalk
it rose up

bark of rough ridges
flecked red
My father's hands

coaxed the new tree
stroked its shiny skin
where it was smooth

as if he   alone
could bring blossoms
to bright stars

as if he   alone
could fill the bower
with flaming flowers

he who emigrated
from the dry earth
of Kiev

where his father's body
moldered in a cemetery
There were no buds there—

~

My mother revered the crabapple
and when it blossomed
she would stand

beneath its brimming arbor
hoping like Hera
that she might be gifted

a golden apple
and live
in The Garden of Hesperides

She would map the veins
of intricate branches
with her fingers

sing into the blue air
between blossoms
sweet   satin   blossoms

The tree grew   taller
it's arbor our shade   my sanctuary
a sacred space

in which to wait
for the plum sky   of dusk
after a hard rain

-for my brother

Hidden

under the old porch
pine boards worn and splintered
there were always spiders

their long wispy legs
the color of cool lake water
a translucent taupe

fragile and feathery
I retracted at their touch
I didn't understand their ways

Perhaps my mother saw
me as the spider
weaving my own web

traversing my winding
threaded pathways
alone

In quiet twilight she stood
over the white porcelain sink
prism light from the lamp above

pouring down
over her eyes
like a hundred little revelations

One of them might bring her closer to me

On My Father's Yahrzeit

I light the small white candle—

hot air hisses in the radiator,
the refrigerator's gnawing whine.

Outside, a heavy pine
drops its needles

leaving prints like fossils
on fresh snow.

In the brittle birch
a black-capped chickadee,

her voice
piercing icy air.

I remember winter dawns like this,
windows rimed with frost.

I stood by you while you stirred
porridge to a golden gruel,

Mozart's Eine Kleine Nachtmusik
floating on fragrant air.

Violet dawn,
first hints of orange sun

bleed into the horizon
like a bruise.

If Only

When there is a full moon
or a harvest moon   yellow and mottled

when there is a sliver of moon
sharp as a silver knife

a shard of white light
cast out into the night

when the grass is yellow   rusting
when leaves turn over   and the grape vines wither

when the sun is low   and wan
when it scorches the earth

when it is eclipsed
and the earth goes black

Long after her death
I will wish

that my mother had been freed
of the yellow walls

of our old split level
that she could have walked

calmly away
from the turquoise kitchen

apron trailing behind her in the grass
that she could have walked

calmly away
into the moonrise

and left a path
for me

August 22

My mother is
somnolent
in this hot room

You are my sunshine, my only...
my song hangs on humid air

only a few weeks ago
she could fill in the blanks

August 23

I know about the build-up
of proteins   Amyloid Beta and Tau
a shriveling of neurons
networks unwinding
grim clockwork

I hardly know my mother now;
she calls out in a high-pitched whine
I have never heard before

Susan tells me, she had a bad night.

There were dark dreams
but I don't know what they were

she can't remember—
perhaps hard memories embodied
in shadows on vague night air.

Susan said, she was flailing in the bed.

Her head banging the wall
her eyes   empty seashells.

August 24

Last night I dreamt of mermaids
  in the surf
    on the white

wild mane of the waves
  and floating mussels
    with no flesh

no byssus attached

August 27

My mother
smaller today

shrinks back   into dust
of dry stalks   in potted plants

her voice fades into cicadas
the night's thrum

August 30

She drinks ginger-pumpkin soup
from a large mug
with two handles

hot liquid runs over the edge
I stroke her hand
Mom, use your spoon so you don't burn yourself

Outside dark clouds collide
She fumbles with her spoon
and asks: Ruthie, what should I do now?

August 31

Dinner time in assisted living—
kernels of corn

small bits of chicken
scattered   a stained napkin

the flotsam and jetsam
of this wrecked ship

small black olives
dot a white dinner plate

an abstract of the day's monotony
pitiless   fruitless

September 2

My mother is 98 now.

Will I grieve
as if I were not
expecting death?

September 8

My brother and I
are prepared

we have bought
the Urn Garden Plot

C North
next to the stone wall

which might hold back
harsh winter   snow

the last in the row
where the katsura grows

scents the air
with burnt sugar

and drops its small
ochre hearts

November 10

The geese rise at once
through smoke-red sun
churning up the twilight sky

weaving a dark braid
against a bank
of steep slate clouds

I imagine the pond
where they have lingered
among pearl white water lilies

Here on this bark brown shore
November's light
dimming

I see their shadows still
scattered leaves
on a wind-blown pond

November 16

I'm not usually here
in the morning

I hoped
to sit with her

eggs cold
small bits spread out on the plate

Mary tries to give her a teaspoon
of morning meds

but she cries out
I try too

no meds today
her eyes are closing

her hair still wet
from this morning's shower

her mother always said
hair is a woman's shining glory

today, mother
it is yours.

December 2

Today I searched for your eyes—

You were silent
when I said my name,

the name you bequeathed me
from your mother.

You were fragile,
a brittle eggshell.

You could hold a world
in your white orb,

7000 pores letting in the air.
You have carried me

and now I am your history.
I heard your voice

when I was still a part of you,
your amniotic fluid feeding me.

Now I feed you, a tiny bird
sipping from a silver spoon,

the simple soup I made for you,
my offering.

December 3

I have been with you
for several hours
your breathing   rapid

arms flailing
I don't know if you are
reaching for me

or out   into the sea
seeking a waving anemone
purple   free

December 13

Shivering
we bury your ashes
near the stone wall

the earth just soft enough
to open for you
receive you

as you deserve
where the weeping cherry
will unfurl its tender blossoms

in spring
where the heron will split
the azure summer air

into ribbons of light
until they fade
into autumn night

your burdens flown

February 14

I cried when I dropped the teacup
robin's egg blue

shattered shards of china
on my kitchen floor

it was yours

Haiku in Spring

Sun fills white curtains
thrum of bumblebees hovers
morning   bloom by bloom

Our Garden in Cote St. Luc

I could take you back
to where the bearded irises grew

in a rowdy yellow row
in green air

heady with dusty pollen
where you would come

with your scissors
to snip the coral peonies

sticky with sweet syrup
black ants feasting

on their whorled petals
swarming the sand hills

they always seemed
to know what to do—

I wonder if you too
admired the ants

their intuitive order
synchronized design—

I could return you
to where the raspberries grew wild

along the wooden fence
give you back

the flush of your cheeks
in high summer

the round and rose
of ripe pomegranates

On Rio Grande Beach After My Mother's Death

My shadow and my mother's merged
on shimmering sand
we are tilting into the light

driftwood petrified   gleaming white
a deposit of whelk   ibis circling
my shadow and my mother's merged

my voice in the wind
I can speak   but she can't hear
on shimmering sand

crimson-lipped leaves of a sea grape
open into briny morning
we are tilting into the light

I am searching her glow
in the sheen of every iridescent shell
my voice in the wind   sea stars dead

yet the flesh seems so alive
my shadow and my mother's merged
we are tilting into the light

II:

TO PLANT A LUPINE AT
TWILIGHT IN THE COMPANY
OF THE EARTHWORM

In the Absence of Birds – Bryce Canyon, Utah

There's an unnatural quiet
between the bleached stones

white light leaks into cracks
not even a scrabble

of weightless claws
on the sandstone cliffs

clouds empty of beak and wing
feather and claw

only shadows
apparitions

dying in fluid flight
blown by the wind

carried up and over the world
the birds have betrayed

silence in the forest of pinyon and fir
mourning on the mountain

Arlington Street, May, 2020.

A still shot—

pavement wet   silent
some black birds on the wire

restaurants   dark
chairs turned over tables

no one moves
between the red brick walls

and locked shop doors
branch shadows   black

on glossy chrome
raw air whines through

fences and dead leaves
even as weeping willows

deliver their lime buds
to the damp   fog-filled air

The Hawk

A sharp-shinned hawk hunts,
her wings severing green air.
The goldfinch shivers.

Post-surgery Blues

Sack of brittle bones
rattling down the stairs
hugging the railing

attempt after attempt
to grasp
with a frozen hand

I can hardly hold a pen now
I can't play the black keys
can't play the blues

We are one now
the hurt
the hobbled

the downcast
the disabled

We are each other's witness
each other's shadow

Ice After a Storm

envelops everything
brittle glass
slender slick branches

bred together
they know their own rattling
chattering like magpies

interlaced they lie
across white air
a silver black abstract

I shudder
in chill crusty morning
awed by the cold fist of sun

and how small I am
standing here
under the great loud beeches

like a girl in the circus crowd
the wild universe
whirling around me

Life in the Pandemic

A hundred sparrows
gather in the firs   flutter

against each other
feathers bronze   umber

their chatter
fills the lilac sky

I long to join them
but I am alone

for now
this is all there is

A History of Despair

When the impulse came
it drove you
despair calling   *No Exit*

Suicide was an option

the disembodied voice
of the wind
rising to a howl

words lifted
from memory
leaves from another season

another country
the generations   manifold
the impulse hammered out

from the horror   you knew
despair   hard
a specter in the night   harrowing

moonlight bone cold
and white
home   an empty drum

It was an option

unconscious of its origin
death could be the end
of unbearable exile

sadness   bare   borne
when it's once been an option
on some level

it could always be an option

By the Fence With the Grey Horse

That day of light
that day I saw her mane
wild as a cattail

I stopped
at the chain link fence
each metal diamond

casting shadowed patterns
over the horse's coat
grey and glimmering

she came to me
lifted her long   swan-like neck
to nuzzle my chest

out of my pocket
I pulled a fragrant apple
she cracked it

with large yellow teeth
murmured to the field
green as ripe lime

my skin shivered   delight coursing down
her coat
rippling in sunlight

She sidled up
close to me   searched
my sticky hands

I wanted to hold her
move into the pasture
with her

while a slight breeze
stroked
the shimmering grasses

Crystal Lake

I carry the lake's serenity
undulating water

changing   rearranging
we suggest each other

This time
I am mirror

cool water over stone
self   submerged

A heron lifts off   soars
azure feathers   glimmer

The wind speaks
I shiver with the beat

counterpoint   counterpoint

A Burdock Leaf, After Janet Malcolm's Photographs

Each moment   the measure
of fiber and tissue

the white space
left   after the leaf is eaten
by insects

the negative of green
is the empty space   seen
then disappeared

the body and the shadow
what's here and what's not
sinews tied   let loose

Any burdock leaf
is more   than what it is not

its holes and ragged edges
are signs
of first   becoming
then   unravelling

On the Eating Disorders Unit

When she enters
thin as an eggshell

only dust is disturbed
floating on a slim raft of sunlight.

I knock on her hard shell,
searching for light

in the dark
hollows of her bones.

Her pulse
is slowing down.

Cold begins to settle,
making a home

in her porous bones,
in her empty house.

Humanity Legally Challenged

Teresa L. Todd... an elected official, government lawyer and single mother in a desert border region near Big Bend National Park...pulled over ...to help Central American migrants... was arrested...

The New York Times, May 10, 2019

She stopped to give them warmth
water   to dispel fear
they are just kids

Along the blacktop
cactus grows tall
erect   dagger spines
border guards   dogs

She said they were lost
she went to be their eyes
to shield   to guide
she stopped so they could rest

Arid soil in drought
water so low
dripping slow

She stopped to wipe away
the dust on their eyelids
the dust in their dry mouths

She stopped to heal

White dust covers the
window of a cruiser
taken in cuffs   like wraiths
they disappeared
into the cold desert night

This Simple Plum, *Prunus domestica*

In my hands
the goddess of plums
peel taut

pulled tight as a drum
purple of dusk's dome
peeling back the cover

on crimson flesh
summer's shameless striptease
loosening fibers

binding pulp to skin
sweet sap
running down my chin

This simple plum has come
from summer dust
from humble hands

I hold its succulence
offering of the sun
of the rain

as if the air were not thinning
as if the rivers were not flooding

and we could be here
forever with the plum tree
delivering fruit to the barrel

His Journey

He is a wraith
passing
through hunger

sliding seamlessly
a thin blade
slicing the air

dizzy   numb
his days are
easier this way

mastery over pain
postponing dawn
his family aches for him

he lets them see only thinness
while the shadow
barely breathes

In This Mood, After Robin Becker

Loss bares its bones
your thin hand veined and trembling

a fern in sharp wind

My face mask blunts the scent of lilacs
willow leaves lance pollen-green air

snowdrops open into reluctant spring

Moonlight reveals the wounds of day
high winds shatter another tree

cherry blossoms land silently

Life Cycle

Each second an unveiling
rich black tuber

coaxed
into thin green air

red-winged blackbird
trilling in bleached bullrushes

her eggs   will break
and the nest   fall into dust

and the nest   fall into dust
her eggs will break

trilling in bleached bullrushes
red-winged blackbird

into thin green air
coaxed

rich black tuber
each second an unveiling

Wild Turkeys

A host of dark creatures
harmonious in their habit

wing by wing
claw by claw
their great bodies

a long black string
undulating the yellowed grass

I envy their straight path
the uncomplicated walk
the low cold sun

Wind Poem

To be the wind
blowing over damp rock
and sodden earth

over the bones and marrow
of crow and possum
on their path back to ash

rising above the rank odor
of fallen leaves lingering
under moldering moss

If I were the wind
I would not need
the affection of coupling

but I am one who longs
and longing's
full of disappointment

if I could be still
I would stand alone
and let the sun warm and fill this vessel

To a Monarch in San Miguel de Allende

You have come
three thousand miles
under the clementine sun

gliding on waves of wind
in the higher reaches of air
to settle

on this flaming Mexican sunflower
milkweed growing in the spaces
between tender stems

Everything depends on vanilla scented
inflorescence   of crimson and purple
Fibonacci design

When you were a caterpillar
you searched diminishing fields
for milky sap

In the lightness of your being
I see our impending demise

We are as close
as a stamen to its petal
as the seed pod to its host

I circle you
like ripples in a quiet pond
kaleidoscope wings   staccato strokes

I hold my breath
before your gloss
ten thousand shadows attach

Beech Trees in Fall, Oil on Canvas
by Christian Rohlfs

in 1937 the Nazis condemned his work as degenerate.

Lush leaves   blade-chiseled
in crimson and ochre
alive

in the space
between beeches
swirling flames swallowing

silver bark   brushing
the cobalt sky
taupe trunks

knotted   tethered
to the dark earth
of forest floor

I know their story
what the blue light
behind them reveals

gnarled trees
growing in the midst
of horror

A Balm for Sadness

Rain gathered
in the white vase

I left out after watering

rain that flowed
over lilac   andromeda
a heady scent—

I will save this water
alchemy of cloud and mist

cool harvest of sky
for the next dry blooms

hear its music spill back
into black earth

To Plant a Lupine at Twilight in the Company of the Earthworm

I

Dig
down
into the dark

naked hands
embedded

let your fingers
make the hole

wide and full
give berth

to roots   let them
wind and spread

a tangle
of hair lined ropes

II

Lumbricina—slime and moisture
slithers smoothly   on their belly

rough with setae
that bristle
protect   move them

Do not interrupt their rounds.

III

Gently   firmly envelop
the tender seedlings of Lupinus
which you have brought

to this moment
micro-bonnets folded
clusters of purple velvet

Sweep in the earth
Wait   with the patience of trees
for full flowering—

You have planted immortality

III:

ANOTHER HAIKU IN SUMMER

A Mother's Journey

You were nub of heart
essence of the word—

I carried you deep within me
your slender lungs
reaching for air

each glimmering line
linking bone to tendon
action to response

And I   always on my journey

In the way of silkworms
I wove silken thread
the warp and weft

morning and night
substance from inchoate being
and carried you

a slim new reed
raw and tender
to wave and bend in wind

but never wilt
I gave what I found
nurtured what needed me

You were
nub of heart
essence of the word

Poem in Utero

Like a reed I grew
groped and grasped
for my strength

waved and bent in wind
but never wilted
I slaked my thirst

from wet clay and riverbed
needing just a flash of sunlight
photosynthesis complete

Haiku in August

Rain barrel empty,
no grapes on the wooden trellis.
Where are my children?

For My Daughter, Simone

Shadow   in dark night
light   on lilacs

an amber peach   ripe on a summer branch
you flourish

my daughter
now a woman

an abundance
a field   full of cattails

the dancer   who stands upright
whose fire burns bright

Parc Lafontaine

When we were young
we lay on velvet grass
folding in   upon each other
stillness almost complete

our touch was tender
as the paper-white wings
of a moth   opening
closing   pulsating together

known by what is left
after wings   shift air
slightly shaking
the long stems of yarrow

Longing hangs   in the air
like an echo
palpable   only
by its visceral insistence

We know longing
by its absence of fulfillment

The painting you did

of the cobalt sea
just before you moved away

how you allowed the fence to fall
down gently around the dunes
bent it like the body

of an old woman
allowed the wood to splinter
where storms had frayed

the slats and the wire
between them   mangled
in the violet hues

reflected off the purple gazebo
tall grasses   pale   pliant
waving in salt breeze

you captured my longing
to stop
there at the edge

of the ocean
and not
take another step

leaving our long
late shadows
on the alabaster sand

-for Emma

For My Husband

When you are lost
I move into the depths
to touch you

I am blind in your darkness
I feel the lines of our years
I say what I know

Are we made of ancient dust
ash of bone
fossils embedded in stone?

I don't know if you hear me
with the wind outside
and the wild red leaves   brushing

against each other's skin
that you are brilliant as Sirius
that you are cool water

to my wilting wildflower
The years unfold our bodies
into air   unravel the threads

that connect us to the earth
I have come   full with desire
to touch   to hold

to find the fire   between us

Tanka

In the shape of your
smile, incandescent on
olive skin, a slim
sliver of moon slides, cosmic
behind coal black midnight clouds

-for Simone

Haiku in Fall

Morning opens to
guitar notes humming. You strum
me today's story.

-for Avi

After the Fire in Mesa Verde

Two yellow birds
share a spare   split branch

in the pinyon pines
blackened   gnarled

in white arid air
where there were flames

hot enough
to have rent the limb   in two

Between bare stalks
an indigo sky   burns

firs carved down
to the thinnest filaments

A forest bloomed here—

Now   juniper berries cast
a dusty blue   hue   onto white light

an antelope jackrabbit leaps
bark-brown parabolas

across freshly grown brush
brimming with sunflower gold

scarlet bugler and larkspur
filling the empty space where

golden eagles brushed their wild wings
against an infinite sky

When you visit

rain rushes the air
and in the space

between us
words tumble down

like water over stones.
We disappear into

each other,
wild words tumbling.

Rain washes over us
cooling everything

Night comes
and wraps us in quiet.

-for Emma

Poem Written in My 69th Year

I stand beneath   the bowing beech
new buds attach
rust red gills   breathe   the heavy air

laden with methane and ozone
in a nest   of thin branches
dark braided vines

whose geometry makes me dizzy—

I bend to slim shoots
wrapped in silken fiber
tended   by a scarlet sun

this heat   we know
this heat   we ignore
I raise my eyes

to the darkening dome
above me   seeking
a path to restore

Scents of musk and rot
rise   from the darkness below

from the warming earth
the drying soil
where decay   meets desire

Poem for My Son, Avi

The supreme question about a work of art is out of how deep a life does it spring.

- James Joyce, Ulysses

It is spring
roots stir in the earth
I hear our words
our talk of James Joyce

and the music
that moves us
our walks
near the lake   light on water

You eat ripe avocado   with your hands
green flesh   lush
fat purple blueberries straight
from the green paper box

unwashed   the raw
wild with desire
sunlight
on your chestnut hair

a crystal sways
in the kitchen window
jade amber   light
You stand as you

always have
while I spice
stir
a fragrant sauce

The Sheepdog

I have been watching over
the house across the street
for some time,
the wooden shingles

losing their color,
peeling down to grey,
pale and dead as concrete,
occasional melancholic guitar notes

sliding out a window
to hang on thick humid air.
The house has always been bedraggled,
the porch collapsing a little more every day.

Once there were lilies,
stalks of Prussian blue delphinium
and speckled foxgloves,
their colors so alive they popped like a circus tent.

Now the path around the back
where the train runs
is thick with burdock leaves
in every stage of decomposition.

I'm concerned
about the state of the old sheepdog
dragging his dwindling body,
all fur covered sticks

sweeping the dirt
with his long ragged tail
lagging
shiftlessly behind.

Traveling in Colombia, 2017

Omar says:

There were always bullets—

In Salento
bloated   villager bodies
floated on the back

of the dark thick river
skin unfolding   molting
shedding its color

tattoos   of their lives
On Sunday mornings
the priest dragged

his black robes
through dust
out of the white church

blessed the souls   deposited
like silt
along the riverbanks

Do not worry, he said,
God will protect you

In Salento's torrid heat
I see the killing
everywhere

tin roofs roast in searing sun
black   waxy   vines
creep along the walls

of hot houses
bougainvillea
fuchsia puffs   dried blood

Another Haiku in Summer

In each other's light
in darkness, apart and near
we are fireflies

-for Emma

Love Poem

I wish I could have you
this way
just for a moment

quiet evening
our hands entwined
skin touching skin

under the twilight sky
full of swallows
their slim pointed wings

strobing the violet light
over us
into a fugue

A Simple Walk

There is   a silence
with us

it hovers
like wings

we gather it
in our hands

the workers toil
in heat

grinding
the cement mixer

blue jays attack
in the trees

you bend your head
to mine   to listen

I reach for you
between   our bodies

our history
fills   the crevices

A silence
with us

-for my husband

New York City Subway

Steam from metal grates
heel of her red stilettos
caught in the steel slats

On the Hills of the Golan, Two Worlds

To the east a column
of sand-colored tanks on maneuvers

crawls like a rattlesnake
silent   ready

Pulled from their lives
young men in dusty helmets

almost invisible
inch along

the chalk-white path
where heat burns

through cactus   in waves
of withering light

To the west
burgundy vineyards

glow in citrine sun
lined up in long neat rows

of woody vines
and claret florets

lush as they were
in the time of Moses

when from the Valley of Eschol
came a cluster of grapes

so large that it was borne
between two upon a staff *

Hot light spreads
like mist across the valley

where oranges hang
in searing mountain sun

so ripe
they might burst

      * (Numbers 13:23)

After the Doctor's Call

A last rose hardened
to an icy nub   fuchsia
pinned under silver frost

my breath comes fast
a turn in the stomach
one muscle   tightening   at a time

we sit in our usual places
at the table
in deepening dusk

I arrange my food
into small hills
and on your plate   rivulets

this hard punch
and the air   so thin
so thin

Winter Dawn

I remember a time
when we were without experience,
when we knew the pace
of each other's heartbeat,

the way we know
the smell of wet earth
and the whistling of wind
through the eaves

of this old wooden house,
before we were embedded,
watching each other
for signs.

I want only to lie beside you
while thin white clouds drift across the sun.
Each year the snow
will cover the splintered porch rails,

a dried oak leaf
or a shred of brown grass hanging on.
What do we really know?
How can we assume?

Summer and My Mother

Her garden—
the iris

unfolding furls
of violet

strokes of sun-soaked yellow
on lanced petals

shadows of plum
on heavy honeysuckle

Her voice weaving
through peonies

floating on summer
and heat waves

I plant the shoots
pack   dark   soil   around the roots

my voice   her voice
my hands   her hands

ACKNOWLEDGMENTS

A hearty thank you to Gloria Mindock, editor of Červená Barva Press, for being an inspiration, for believing in me and publishing my book; and thank you as well, to all at the press who brought this book to fruition.

My deep gratitude goes to Eric Hyett, for his wonderful workshops, unbounded kindness and for tirelessly critiquing every poem in this book, thus making me a far better poet.

I thank my poetry critique group, Deborah Leipziger and Lawrence Kessenich for their years of thoughtful criticism and warm support; I am grateful for our time together.

Gratitude goes to my teachers, Barbara Helfgott Hyett, for her amazing workshops and brilliant insights, and to Ellen Bass, Marie Howe, David Baker and Dorianne Laux for their terrific courses, through which I have deepened my knowledge of the music and craft of poetry.

Thank you to my wonderful family, Mark, Emma, Simone and Avi who have read every poem in this book and have never ceased to encourage me.

~

Acknowledgments are due to the editors of the following journals, in which the poems in this book, first appeared, sometimes in different forms:

Amethyst: "To Plant a Lupine at Twilight in the Company of the Earthworm," "Lifecycle"

Constellations: "Hidden," "Traveling in Salento, Colombia," "Winter Dawn," "Wind Poem," "Crystal Lake"

Haiku Universe: "New York City Subway," "Haiku in August"

Ibbetson Street: "On the Eating Disorders Unit," "Winter's Sparrow," "On the Hills of the Golan – Two Worlds," "Perpetual Twilight," "On My Father's Yahrzeit," "If Only," "Days of My Mother," "Park Lafontaine," "Ice After a

Storm," "His Journey," "Our Garden in Cote St. Luc," "The Sheepdog", "A Balm for Sadness"

Lily Poetry Review: "Poem Written in my 69th year"

Lyrical Somerville: "If I had Wings," "A Mother's Journey"

Muddy River Poetry Review: "Beech Trees in Fall," "For My Father," "A Burdock Leaf," "Light Comes Slowly, "This Simple Plum, Prunus domestica," "By the Fence With the Grey Horse," "For My Husband," "Wind Chimes," "A History of Despair"

Poetry Super Highway: "On Rio Grande Beach After My Mother's death"

Soul Lit: "Love Poem," "Trying to Help Migrants on the Road"

the Aurorean: "Days of My Mother: Nov. 20"

The Bagel Bard Anthology: "Autumn Lament," "In the Absence of Birds"

Voices of the Earth: The Future of the Planet III: "To a Monarch in San Miguel"

Writing in a Woman's Voice: "The Painting You Did"

ABOUT THE AUTHOR

Ruth C. Chad is a psychologist who lives and works in the Boston area. Her poems have appeared in the *Aurorean, Connection, Psychoanalytic Couple and Family Institute of New England, Constellations, Ibbetson Street, Montreal Poems, Muddy River Poetry Review, Lily Poetry Review, Amethyst Poetry Review, Writing in a Woman's Voice*, and others. Her chapbook, "The Sound of Angels", was published by Červená Barva Press in 2017. Ruth was nominated for a Pushcart prize in 2021.